CB7725

D1074475

THE BABY IN MOMMY'S TUMMY

Written by Michelle Cole

Illustrated by ISz

THE BABY IN MOMMY'S TUMMY
by Michelle Cole
Illustrations by ISz

Editing by Gregory F.A. Pierce
Design and typesetting by Patricia A. Lynch

acta

ACTA Publications
4848 North Clark Street
Chicago, Illinois 60640
(800) 397-2282
www.actapublications.com

Library of Congress Control Number: 2017932800
ISBN: 978-0-87946-591-9

Printed in the United States of America by Total Printing Systems
Year 30 29 28 27 26 25 24 23 22 21 20 19 18 17
Printing 15 14 13 12 11 10 9 8 7 6 5 4 3 2 First

♻ Text printed on 30% post-consumer recycled paper

"Before I shaped you in the womb,
I knew all about you."

Baby is living inside of your mother;

Baby will be your new sister or brother.

But Baby must grow more before you can meet

So let's learn how Baby is changing each week.

Like an open book, you watched me grow…

...from conception to birth.

You'd like to hold Baby, but right now you can't.

At six weeks or so Baby's the size of an ant.

Hold your hand on your heart. Do you feel the thump, thump?

The small heart of Baby can already pump!

All the stages of my life…

...were spread out before you.

On your belly's a button, but what is it for?

　　You were joined there to Mommy before you were born.

It helped you to grow by allowing in food.

　　At week number eight, Baby eats this way too.

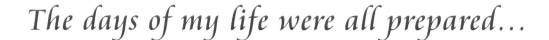

The days of my life were all prepared…

...before I'd even lived one day.

Give your arms and your legs a good shake and a wiggle.

At week number nine, Baby might start to wriggle.

These kicks are too small to be felt or be seen.

Baby's as small as a bumbling bee.

We see that God has carefully placed…

...each part of the body right where he wanted it.

Ten weeks have passed; can you count up to ten?

Here's how to do it with feet or with hands.

Count your ten fingers or count your ten toes.

Baby at ten weeks should have all of those.

His works are perfect…

...and the way he works is fair and just.

Your hair—is it brown? Is it blond, black, or red?

Guess, at fourteen weeks, what's on Baby's head?

Hairs may be growing and Baby grows faster.

Baby's the size of a furry pet hamster!

God pays attention to you…

...even numbering the hairs on your head!

At week number twenty, we're half through our wait.

An ultrasound picture can show Baby's traits.

We might learn if a girl or a boy is inside,

Or instead we might wait to be later surprised.

God created human beings…

...created them male and female.

At twenty-three weeks, it's a great time to talk,

 Or whisper or giggle, or sing out or squawk.

Are you able to hear yourself? Baby may too!

 With two ears that work, Baby listens like you.

Ears that hear and eyes that see…

...we get our basic equipment from God!

At week twenty-seven, would you be surprised

That Baby might open his or her eyes?

Soon little Baby will look up at you

And like to be read to and play peek-a-boo.

Before you saw the light of day…

…I had holy plans for you.

When it's week thirty, sweet Baby will grow
    To the size of a bunny or maybe more so.
If you put your hand upon Mommy's tummy,
    Baby may move and it may feel funny!

You know exactly how I was made, bit by bit…

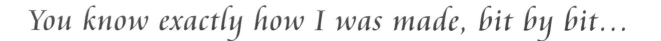

…how I was sculpted from nothing into something.

At thirty-five weeks, your new sister or brother

Will be even bigger inside of your mother.

Baby's so big that when you try to sit

Upon Mommy's lap, you might not even fit!

Oh yes, you shaped me first inside, then out…

…you formed me in my mother's womb.

When all forty weeks have passed one another,

    At last you will meet your new sister or brother.

So say "thank you" to God, who lives up above.

    Our family will grow—and so will our love.

I thank you, High God—you're breathtaking...

...Body and soul, I am marvelously made!

The Scripture quotes in this book are from *The Message* by Eugene Peterson, a translation of the Bible from the original ancient texts into contemporary language. They are found in the passages that follow.

Genesis 1:26-28

God spoke: "Let us make human beings in our image,
    make them reflecting our nature
So they can be responsible for the fish in the sea,
    the birds in the air, the cattle,
And, yes, Earth itself,
    and every animal that moves on the face of Earth."
God created human beings;
    he created them godlike,
Reflecting God's nature.
    He created them male and female.
God blessed them:
    "Prosper! Reproduce! Fill Earth! Take charge!
Be responsible for fish in the sea and birds in the air,
    for every living thing that moves on the face of Earth."

Deuteronomy 32:1-4

Listen, Heavens, I have something to tell you.
> Attention, Earth, I've got a mouth
> > full of words.
My teaching, let it fall like a gentle rain,
> my words arrive like morning dew,
Like a sprinkling rain on new grass,
> like spring showers on the garden.
For it's GOD's Name I'm preaching—
> respond to the greatness of our God!
The Rock: His works are perfect,
> and the way he works is fair and just;
A God you can depend upon, no exceptions,
> a straight-arrow God.

Psalm 139:13-16

Oh yes, you shaped me first inside, then out;
> you formed me in my mother's womb.
I thank you, High God—you're breathtaking!
> Body and soul, I am marvelously made!
> I worship in adoration—what a creation!
You know me inside and out,
> you know every bone in my body;
You know exactly how I was made, bit by bit,
> how I was sculpted from nothing
> > into something.
Like an open book, you watched me grow
> from conception to birth;
> all the stages of my life
> > were spread out before you,
The days of my life all prepared
> before I'd even lived one day.

Proverbs 20:12

Ears that hear and eyes that see—
    we get our basic equipment from God.

Jeremiah 1:5

"Before I shaped you in the womb,
    I knew all about you.
Before you saw the light of day,
    I had holy plans for you."

1 Corinthians 12:18

As it is, we see that God has carefully placed each part of the body right where he wanted it.

Matthew 10:29-31

"What's the price of a pet canary? Some loose change, right? And God cares what happens to it even more than you do. He pays even greater attention to you, down to the last detail—even numbering the hairs on your head! So don't be intimidated by all this bully talk. You're worth more than a million canaries."

Luke 12:6-17

"What's the price of two or three pet canaries? Some loose change, right? But God never overlooks a single one. And he pays even greater attention to you, down to the last detail—even numbering the hairs on your head! So don't be intimidated by all this bully talk. You're worth more than a million canaries"

ABOUT THE AUTHOR

Exploring the living world and learning about its creator inspire me. My undergraduate studies at the University of Dallas, a liberal arts university, encouraged my pursuit of these two passions while I earned a B.S. in biology and a B.A. in theology. I continued my education at Texas A&M University, earning a Ph.D. in biology. I am currently a wife and mother in Houston, Texas.

During my own pregnancies, I enjoyed the many resources for new parents that teach about the awe-inspiring development that occurs before a baby is born, but I lamented the lack of similar resources for younger family members. Despite many siblings being close in age, young children's books on prenatal development are rare, especially ones that display God as the author of this new life. To fill this niche, I wrote *The Baby in Mommy's Tummy*. I hope this book will help young children—especially new big brothers and big sisters—to bond with their unborn brothers and sisters and see God's creating hand.

This book is dedicated to my children. You are wonderfully made!

ABOUT THE ILLUSTRATOR

Call me ISz. I chose this name and identity because it expresses that which simply "is"—our immediate and active life-state and timeless connection with all things.

It is from this connection, this oneness, that my images emerge—from the simple, childlike drawings in this book to my pen and ink drawings in my book *We the Little People* to my larger works of art, including paintings and sculpture on display in galleries in the U.S. and internationally and in my studio in Chicago where all visitors are always welcome. They can also be seen online at www.iszart.com.

Those participating in my imagery—especially children—bring their own unique perspectives and can manipulate the many elements in my work in profoundly individual ways. In doing so they can begin to see the endless possibilities of who we human beings are and what we can become. This experience will, I trust, leave a spiritual "afterimage" that fades into a realization that we are one family in a vast universe, a universe only fully explored and understood together.

BESTSELLING CHILDREN'S BOOKS FROM ACTA

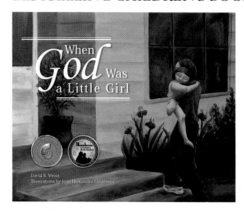

Fourth Annual Illumination Awards
Enduring Light Gold Award

2016 Catholic Press Association Book Awards
First Place, Children's Books

2016 Mom's Choice Award®
Gold Medal, Children's Books

2014 Moonbeam Children's Book Award
Gold Medal, Religion/Spirituality

2014 Nautilus Books Award
Silver Medal Children's Picture Book

This tale sparkles with the exuberant joy of God's creative energy revealed through the metaphor of a little girl doing an art project—an explosion of color and shapes, glue and glitter. Girls, whose outer appearance varies in age and culture throughout the book, mirror the uncontainable Love with which God sang the world into being.

32 pages, hardcover

"Before I formed you in the womb, I knew you." These words from Jeremiah 1:5 led Claire Boudreaux Bateman to reflect on God's gifts— the gift of life, the gift of an incredible inner light, the gift of family—regardless of circumstances, struggles, illness, or disability.

36 pages, hardcover

Available from Booksellers or from ACTA PUBLICATIONS
800-397-2282 / www.actapublications.com